The Power of Words and Thoughts

The Power of Words and Thoughts

Emem Ossei

Published by Emem Ossei, 2024.

THE POWER OF WORDS AND THOUGHTS

First edition. August 22, 2024.

ISBN: 979-8227647825

Written by Emem Ossei.

This book is dedicated to my parents Edward and Angela, who encouraged me to read

By Emem Ossei

Introduction: The Journey of Transformation

In the vast tapestry of life, each of us embarks on a unique journey, woven together by experiences, thoughts, and the choices we make. This journey, while deeply personal, is also universal—an intricate dance of triumphs and trials that shapes us into who we are meant to be. As we navigate this path, we often encounter moments of clarity, inspiration, and transformation, where our words and thoughts hold the power to ignite change.

Imagine standing at the edge of a vast ocean, the waves crashing against the shore. Each wave represents a thought—a potential energy waiting to be harnessed. Some waves are gentle, whispering encouragement, while others may crash tumultuously, urging us to confront our fears. It is in this dynamic interplay between thought and action that we discover our true selves and unlock the potential that lies within.

Reflecting on my own journey, I recall a pivotal moment when I realized the profound impact my words had on my life and the lives of those around me. In a time of uncertainty, I found solace in the power of positive affirmations, which transformed my outlook and inspired me to take action toward my dreams. This experience ignited a passion within me—a desire to explore the depths of our thoughts and the energy they project into the world.

Throughout this book, we will explore the profound influence of our words and thoughts, examining how they shape our realities and the world around us. Each chapter will unfold like a new horizon, introducing you to powerful metaphors and relatable stories that highlight the importance of resilience, creativity, and authenticity. Together, we will delve into the lives of remarkable individuals—firefighters, artists, navigators—and uncover the lessons they impart.

As you embark on this journey of self-discovery, I invite you to reflect on your own experiences and engage in thought-provoking activities that encourage growth and introspection. Consider the moments when a word or thought shifted your perspective or propelled you forward. You hold the brush to your own canvas, the compass to guide your ship, and the fire to ignite your passion. The power to transform your life lies within you.

Let us begin this adventure together, embracing the challenges and celebrating the victories that await. Approach this journey with an open mind and heart, allowing for growth and transformation throughout your reading experience. Remember, your journey is not merely about reaching a destination; it is about the beauty of the transformation that unfolds along the way.

Chapter 1: The Power of Words

Take time to listen to yourself talk; be critical of what you say. Just as an author dictates into a recorder or a student diligently takes notes in class, reflecting on your speech can unveil powerful insights. The words we speak carry immense energy that affects not just ourselves but also those around us. Even casual remarks made in jest can create a ripple effect in our psyche and that of others. Our pets, too, are influenced by the energy emitted through our words.

Sometimes, we say things without thinking, only to wonder later why those words have such a profound impact on our lives. This is because our words are not merely sounds; they are potent forces of universal energy.

We often underestimate the significance of our speech and the energy it carries. Every time we speak, we project energy into the world. Why not ensure that this energy is positive? Words possess dynamic power; each of us is a powerful universal force with the ability to create. Therefore, refrain from speaking negativity into existence. Positive people naturally articulate positive thoughts. If we have the power to manifest our realities, let's use that ability to spread love, kindness, and compassion.

To spread love into the world, we must pause and reflect before we speak, carefully choosing the energy we contribute to the universe. Visualize the potential impacts of our words, just like a video recording. If negative words slip out, rewind and replace them with positivity. It is our responsibility to fill our universe with loving energy; you are the catalyst for this transformation.

Reflection Prompts:

1. What words do you frequently use that may carry negative energy?

2. How do you feel after speaking positively or negatively?

3. Can you recall a time when your words significantly impacted someone else?

Thought Activity:

Create a "Word Journal" where you document instances of your speech throughout the week. Reflect on the energy behind your words and how they affected you and others.

Conclusion:

Recognize the power within your words. As you become more aware of the energy you project, strive to cultivate positivity in your communication. Your words can create a ripple effect, influencing not only your life but also the lives of those around you.

Chapter 2: The Farmer's Wisdom

In life, we should embody the principles of a farmer. Farmers live by the Law of Reciprocity; they sow seeds and tend to them daily, even when results are not immediately visible. Each morning, they wake up with purpose, nurturing their crops with care. The farmer understands that even during a bad harvest, the act of working diligently is a reward in itself. Eventually, through consistent effort, they will reap a bountiful harvest.

Consider the miracle of life unfolding all around us. At any given moment, someone is being born, while another is passing away; some are experiencing joy, while others face despair. Life is a tapestry of experiences. Each morning, affirm your purpose. Like the farmer, I remind myself daily that today will be amazing. This transformational vocabulary fuels my thoughts and feelings, laying the groundwork for positive reciprocal behavior.

The farmer's routine can serve as a powerful metaphor for our own lives. Just as he tends to his crops with diligence, we must cultivate our thoughts, emotions, and actions to foster growth and positivity. It's essential to recognize that our daily efforts, no matter how small, contribute to the larger picture of our lives. Just as the farmer patiently awaits the fruits of his labor, we too must be patient with ourselves and trust the process of growth.

Furthermore, the farmer teaches us resilience. In times of adversity, when the harvest is poor or the weather is unforgiving, he continues to work, knowing that his efforts will eventually bear fruit. In our lives, challenges and setbacks are inevitable, but they should not deter us from our purpose. Instead, we should embrace these moments as opportunities for learning and growth, trusting that our persistence will lead us to success.

Reflection Prompts:

1. What "seeds" are you currently sowing in your life?

2. How do you maintain a sense of purpose in your daily routine?

3. Can you identify a time when your hard work paid off, even if it took longer than expected?

Thought Activity:

Create a "Growth Plan" where you outline specific goals and the daily actions you will take to nurture them. Monitor your progress over time, reflecting on the lessons learned along the way.

Conclusion:

Embrace the farmer's wisdom as you cultivate your life. Understand that every effort counts, and even in the face of adversity, your dedication will lead to eventual rewards. Trust the process and remain committed to your purpose.

Chapter 3: Negative Thoughts

Negative thoughts can appear suddenly, growing like mushrooms in a damp forest. Though they can bring awareness, they predominantly multiply and spread, infiltrating all aspects of our lives and influencing our behavior. Our negative thinking contributes to the development of a harmful belief system that affects how we treat others, react in relationships, and express love.

What is a thought? It is energy created by our brains, which can be positive, negative, or neutral. This energy flows through us, shaping our beliefs and actions. The more positive energy we foster, the more positivity surrounds us, leading to beneficial interactions and connections.

Do not allow negative thoughts to take root, no matter how small. Tiny thoughts can gather, fermenting within us and weaving themselves into the fabric of our being. Over time, they can weaken the strength of our lives. Therefore, never hold onto negative thoughts.

When negativity arises, reframe it immediately. Transform negative thoughts into positive affirmations, such as "I am worthy" or "Everything will be alright." Positive thoughts foster positive feelings and beliefs, leading to constructive behaviors. Each thought you create has the potential for action and accomplishment. By reframing negative thoughts, you can change the energy surrounding you at any moment.

Just as thoughts are like birds that fly over our heads, we cannot prevent them from appearing, but we can choose not to let them build nests in our minds. We must eradicate negative thoughts before they take hold and become part of our psyche. Allowing negativity to fester can lead to somatic sickness, resulting in anxiety, depression, and other health issues.

To combat this, we must actively confront negative thoughts, treating them as unwelcome guests in our minds. By doing so, we protect our mental space, fostering an environment where positivity can thrive.

Reflection Prompts:

1. What negative thoughts tend to recur in your mind?

2. How do these thoughts affect your daily life and interactions?

3. Can you identify patterns in your negative thinking?

Thought Activity:

Practice daily affirmations by writing down three positive statements about yourself each morning. Repeat them aloud to reinforce positive thinking and counter negative thoughts.

Conclusion:

Recognize the power of your thoughts. By reframing negativity and nurturing positivity, you can transform your mental landscape. Commit to actively challenging negative thoughts and creating a healthier mindset.

Chapter 4: The Football Player's Journey

Life should be viewed as a journey of constant growth, similar to a football player's experience. Often, we impose unrealistic expectations on ourselves regarding success, resulting in stagnation due to the fear of failure. We overlook the small victories necessary to achieve our larger goals.

Consider the story of a football player who aspired to be a superstar. His ultimate goal was fame and recognition, but he focused on making the team first. He reminded himself, "I will enjoy every moment of this process." Though he didn't make the main roster, he joined the practice squad and dedicated himself to improvement, relishing each practice.

As he progressed, he maintained his larger goal while appreciating the small successes along the way. When he was finally activated to play, he caught a touchdown pass, a testament to his hard work and dedication. His journey teaches us to set lofty goals while cherishing the small victories that lead us there.

This player's journey exemplifies the importance of living in the moment. While he aimed for stardom, he found joy in the process, understanding that each practice, each game, and each interaction was part of his growth. By focusing on the present, he cultivated gratitude for every experience, reinforcing his resilience and determination.

As we navigate our paths, we should adopt this mindset. Set ambitious goals, but do not lose sight of the importance of enjoying the journey. Celebrate the small wins, learn from setbacks, and embrace each moment as it comes. This approach not only enriches our lives but also keeps us grounded in our pursuit of success.

Reflection Prompts:

1. What are your biggest goals, and what small victories can you celebrate along the way?

2. How do you stay present and enjoy the journey toward your goals?

3. Can you recall a time when focusing on the moment led to unexpected opportunities?

Thought Activity:

Create a "Victory Log" where you document your small wins each week. Reflect on how these victories contribute to your larger goals and how they make you feel.

Conclusion:

Embrace the journey of growth as a football player does. Celebrate the small victories and remain present in the process. By doing so, you will cultivate resilience and gratitude, paving the way for future successes.

Chapter 5: The Oarsman's Balance

In our fast-paced world, we often lose our sense of self while striving for validation and relevance. The story of the oarsman illustrates this struggle. He loved being on the water and meticulously prepared for his rowing trips. However, over time, he became overconfident and neglected fundamental checks on his boat. When his rudder broke, he found himself adrift, having forgotten the essential tools that guided him.

This tale serves as a powerful reminder that amidst the chaos of modern life, we must not lose sight of our core values and foundational principles. Just as the oarsman forgot to check his rudder, we may overlook the very aspects of our lives that keep us grounded.

Living life in the fast lane can lead us to prioritize superficial achievements over meaningful connections and self-awareness. We often compare ourselves to others, seeking validation through social media and societal expectations. This constant pursuit can cause us to drift away from our true selves.

To find balance, we must regularly check in with ourselves, ensuring that we are aligned with our values and purpose. This includes taking time for self-reflection, evaluating our priorities, and making adjustments as necessary. Just as the oarsman must navigate the waters with intention, we too must steer our lives with clarity and purpose.

Reflection Prompts:

1. What foundational values guide your life decisions?

2. How do you ensure that you remain true to yourself amidst external pressures?

3. Can you identify moments when you felt adrift in your life? How did you regain your direction?

Thought Activity:

Create a "Values Compass" where you list your core values and assess how well your current actions align with them. Reflect on any necessary adjustments to steer back on course.

Conclusion:

Remain grounded in your values as you navigate life's challenges. By regularly checking in with yourself and prioritizing authenticity, you can maintain balance and clarity in your journey.

Chapter 6: The Rapper's Story

In a society where masks are prevalent, we often hide our true selves out of fear of judgment. The story of a talented rapper illustrates this dilemma. Initially, he expressed progressive themes in his music, but as the industry shifted, he felt compelled to conform. He donned the mask of a persona that contradicted his true self, leading him down a path of superficiality and despair.

This rapper's journey is a powerful commentary on the pressures of societal expectations. As he adopted different masks to fit in, he lost sight of his authentic self. The layers of personas he created became suffocating, leaving him feeling disconnected from who he truly was.

However, the story does not end in despair. The rapper eventually realizes that beneath the layers of masks, his authentic self remains. By peeling away these masks, he begins to rediscover his identity, embracing vulnerability and self-acceptance. This transformative process allows him to reconnect with his true passion and purpose.

His journey underscores the importance of authenticity in a world filled with expectations. Rather than conforming to external pressures, we must dare to be ourselves, celebrating our uniqueness. By doing so, we not only liberate ourselves but also inspire others to embrace their true selves.

Reflection Prompts:

1. What "masks" do you wear in your daily life?

2. How do these masks impact your relationships and sense of self?

3. Can you recall a moment when you felt truly authentic? What contributed to that feeling?

Thought Activity:

Engage in a "Mask Removal Exercise" where you list the roles you play in life (e.g., friend, employee, partner) and identify which ones feel authentic and which feel like masks. Reflect on how you can embrace your true self in each role.

Conclusion:

Embrace the journey of authenticity. By shedding the masks that no longer serve you, you can reconnect with your true self. Celebrate your uniqueness and inspire others to do the same.

Chapter 7: Cherishing Relationships

As humans, we often treat our relationships like disposable items. When faced with betrayal or hurt, we may be tempted to throw away connections rather than nurture them. Just as we wouldn't discard our favorite shirt over a stain, we should strive to preserve and repair our relationships, valuing the beautiful experiences shared over time.

Relationships, like cherished items, require care and attention. When difficulties arise, our instinct may be to sever ties, but it is essential to remember the positive memories and experiences that have shaped those connections.

By approaching our relationships with compassion and understanding, we can navigate challenges together, reinforcing the bonds that tie us. Instead of throwing away the proverbial shirt, we can turn it into something new, cherishing the history we have built together.

It is crucial to acknowledge that every relationship will face trials. The key lies in how we respond to these challenges. Rather than allowing one negative experience to overshadow the many positive moments, we must focus on communication, empathy, and forgiveness.

Through nurturing our relationships, we create a supportive network that enriches our lives. We learn from each other, grow together, and ultimately create a tapestry of shared experiences that withstands the test of time.

Reflection Prompts:

1. How do you typically respond to conflict in your relationships?

2. What are some positive memories you cherish with the people in your life?

3. Can you think of a relationship you might want to nurture more intentionally?

Thought Activity:

Write a letter to someone you value, expressing your appreciation for them and reflecting on your shared experiences. Consider sharing the letter with them to strengthen your bond.

Conclusion:

Cherish your relationships as valuable treasures. By approaching them with care, empathy, and understanding, you can foster deeper connections that withstand the test of time.

Chapter 8: The Journey to Positivity

As we move through life, cultivating positivity becomes essential. The journey to positivity is not a destination but a continuous process of self-discovery and growth. Each day presents us with choices to make—choices that can either uplift us or bring us down.

Recognizing the power of our thoughts and words is a crucial step in this journey. By consciously choosing to focus on the positive, we can reshape our experiences and interactions. Affirmations and gratitude practices can help reinforce a positive mindset, allowing us to see the beauty in everyday life.

Embrace the transformative power of positivity. It not only enhances our well-being but also creates a ripple effect in the lives of those around us. When we embody positivity, we attract like-minded individuals, fostering a supportive and uplifting community.

This chapter encourages us to share our positive experiences and inspire others to join them on this journey. It's about building a movement of love, kindness, and support that spreads far beyond ourselves.

Reflection Prompts:

1. What practices do you currently use to cultivate positivity in your life?

2. How do you respond to negative situations? Can you identify areas for improvement?

3. Who inspires you to be more positive, and how can you emulate their influence?

Thought Activity:

Start a "Positivity Jar" where you collect notes of positive experiences, achievements, and affirmations. Review them regularly to reinforce your positive mindset.

Conclusion:

Cultivating positivity is an ongoing journey that requires intentional effort. By embracing positivity and sharing it with others, you can create a ripple effect that transforms your life and the lives of those around you.

Chapter 9: The Importance of Self-Reflection

Self-reflection is a vital tool for personal growth. Taking the time to pause and assess our thoughts, actions, and motivations allows us to gain clarity about our lives and values. Through reflection, we can identify areas for improvement and celebrate our successes.

Encourage yourself and others to set aside regular time for self-reflection, whether through journaling, meditation, or quiet contemplation. This practice fosters self-awareness and empowers individuals to make intentional choices that align with their values and goals.

Self-reflection also invites vulnerability, enabling us to confront our fears and insecurities. By acknowledging our imperfections, we can cultivate compassion for ourselves and others, fostering deeper connections in our relationships.

Reflection Prompts:

1. How often do you engage in self-reflection, and what methods do you use?

2. What insights have you gained from your past reflections?

3. How can self-reflection help you navigate current challenges in your life?

Thought Activity:

Begin a "Reflection Journal" where you write down your thoughts and feelings at the end of each day. Use this space to explore your experiences and track your growth over time.

Conclusion:

Embrace self-reflection as a powerful tool for personal development. By regularly assessing your thoughts and actions, you can cultivate self-awareness and foster deeper connections with yourself and others.

Chapter 10: Overcoming Adversity

Life's challenges are inevitable, but how we respond to them defines our character. Adversity can be a powerful teacher, offering valuable lessons and opportunities for growth. Rather than viewing setbacks as failures, we can reframe them as stepping stones on our journey.

This chapter shares inspiring stories of individuals who have faced significant challenges and emerged stronger. Their resilience serves as a reminder that we are capable of overcoming obstacles and achieving our goals, no matter the circumstances.

Encourage yourself and others to adopt a growth mindset, viewing challenges as opportunities for learning and self-improvement. By embracing adversity, we can cultivate resilience and strength, enabling us to navigate life's ups and downs with grace.

Reflection Prompts:

1. Can you recall a significant challenge you have faced? What did you learn from that experience?

2. How do you typically respond to adversity? Are there strategies you can adopt to improve your resilience?

3. Who in your life inspires you to overcome challenges, and how can you draw strength from their example?

Thought Activity:

Create a "Resilience Map" where you outline past challenges, the lessons learned, and the strengths you gained from each experience. Use this map as a reminder of your ability to overcome adversity.

Conclusion:

Adversity is a natural part of life, and how we respond to it shapes our character. By embracing challenges as opportunities for growth, we can cultivate resilience and strength, paving the way for future successes.

Chapter 11: The Firefighter

In our lives, we often encounter moments that feel like raging fires—situations that demand immediate attention, courage, and resilience. Just as a firefighter rushes into a blaze to extinguish flames and save lives, we too must confront our challenges head-on, armed with determination and a steadfast spirit.

Real-Life Examples: Consider the story of a firefighter named Sarah, who faced an intense wildfire threatening her community. Amidst the chaos, she exemplified calm and focus, leading her team through perilous conditions. Sarah's determination to protect her family and neighbors fueled her courage. Her story is a testament to the power of resilience and the willingness to face adversity head-on.

The role of a firefighter is not merely about battling flames; it is about preparedness, teamwork, and the ability to stay calm amidst chaos. Firefighters train tirelessly, learning to respond quickly and effectively to emergencies. They understand that every fire is unique, requiring a tailored approach to extinguish it. Similarly, in our lives, we must cultivate the skills and mindset necessary to tackle our own personal fires.

Strategies for Resilience:

1. Mindfulness Practices: Take a few minutes each day to practice mindfulness or meditation. Focus on your breath and bring awareness to your thoughts and feelings. This practice can help you remain calm in stressful situations.

2. Building a Support Network: Surround yourself with supportive friends, family, or mentors who can provide encouragement and guidance during tough times. Don't hesitate to reach out for help when needed.

3. Setting Small Goals: Break down larger challenges into smaller, manageable tasks. Each small victory will build your confidence and motivate you to keep pushing forward.

When faced with adversity, it can be easy to feel overwhelmed. However, just as firefighters assess a situation before acting, we must pause to evaluate our challenges. Identify the sources of stress—whether they are external pressures or internal struggles—and develop a strategy to address them.

Reflection Prompts:

1. What are the "fires" in your life that demand your attention right now?

2. How do you typically respond to stressful situations? Are there ways you can improve your approach?

3. Can you recall a time when you faced adversity and emerged stronger? What did you learn from that experience?

Thought Activity: Create a "Firefighter Action Plan" where you identify a current challenge in your life. Outline the steps you will take to confront this challenge, including resources and support systems you can tap into.

Conclusion: Embrace the spirit of the firefighter as you navigate the challenges in your life. By approaching adversity with courage, resilience, and a strategic mindset, you can extinguish the flames of stress and emerge stronger on the other side.

Chapter 12: The Artist

In the canvas of life, each of us is an artist, wielding the brush of our choices and experiences to create a masterpiece. An artist understands the significance of every stroke, every color, and every texture. Similarly, our lives are shaped by the decisions we make and the passion we infuse into our pursuits.

Creative Exercises:

1. Journaling Prompts: Spend 10 minutes each day writing about your emotions—what inspires you, what challenges you face, and how you express yourself. Reflect on the moments that have shaped your identity.

2. Art Projects: Create a piece of art that represents a significant moment in your life. Use colors and symbols that resonate with your experience. This can be painting, drawing, or any medium that speaks to you.

3. Community Involvement: Join a local art class or community project where you can collaborate with others. Engaging with a creative community can inspire new ideas and connections.

An artist does not shy away from imperfections; instead, they embrace them as part of the creative process. Each mistake becomes a lesson, a stepping stone toward mastery. In our lives, we must learn to view our setbacks as part of the journey. Just as a painting evolves over time, so do we.

Exploration of Imperfection:

Consider the famous artist Vincent van Gogh, whose work was often dismissed during his lifetime. Van Gogh embraced his struggles with mental health and transformed them into stunning artworks that resonate with raw emotion. His journey teaches us that embracing imperfections can lead to extraordinary growth and creativity.

The artist's journey is also one of expression. Through their work, they communicate emotions, ideas, and stories. In our own lives, we have the power to express ourselves authentically, sharing our unique perspectives with the world. This requires vulnerability—a willingness to expose our true selves and share our experiences, both beautiful and challenging.

Reflection Prompts:

1. What does being an artist mean to you in the context of your life?

2. How do you express your creativity, and what passions fuel your artistic pursuits?

3. Can you identify a time when you have embraced imperfection as part of your journey? What did you learn?

Thought Activity: Create a "Personal Canvas" where you visually represent your values, passions, and aspirations. Use colors, images, and words to express who you are and what you want to create in your life.

Conclusion:

As you navigate your life's journey, remember that you are an artist. Embrace the process of creation, express your authentic self, and draw inspiration from the world around you. Your life is a masterpiece in the making.

Chapter 13: The Navigator

In the vast ocean of life, each of us is a navigator, charting our course through uncharted waters. A navigator understands the importance of direction, using tools and knowledge to traverse the complexities of the journey ahead. Just as sailors rely on maps and compasses, we too must know our values and goals to steer us through life.

Mapping the Journey:

1. Identify Your Core Values: Take time to list your core values. What principles guide your decisions? Consider how these values shape your goals and aspirations.

2. Set Clear Goals: Break your long-term aspirations into short-term, actionable goals. This can be a combination of personal, professional, and creative objectives.

3. Regular Check-Ins: Schedule weekly or monthly reflections to assess your progress. Are you staying true to your values? Are your actions aligned with your goals?

Navigators face various challenges—storms, currents, and obstacles that threaten to derail their journey. However, they possess the skills to adapt and recalibrate their course.

Similarly, we must be prepared to confront the unexpected and remain flexible in our approach. Life may not always go as planned, but by staying true to our values, we can find our way back on track.

The Importance of Reflection:

Navigators regularly assess their position, reflecting on their progress and adjusting their sails as needed. In our lives, self-reflection is crucial to understanding our emotions, motivations, and desires. By taking time to evaluate our direction, we can make informed choices that align with our true selves.

Methods for Effective Reflection:

1. Journaling: Dedicate time to write about your thoughts, feelings, and experiences. This practice can help clarify your goals and emotions.

2. Meditation: Spend quiet moments in meditation to connect with your inner self. Reflect on your journey and the paths you want to pursue.

3. Mentorship: Seek guidance from mentors who can provide insights based on their experiences. Their perspectives can illuminate your own path.

Reflection Prompts:

1. What direction do you want to take in your life, and how can you ensure you stay on course?

2. How do you assess your progress and make adjustments when challenges arise?

3. Who are your mentors or guides, and how have they influenced your journey?

Thought Activity:

Create a "Life Map" where you outline your goals and the steps you will take to achieve them. Include potential obstacles and strategies for overcoming them, envisioning your journey as a navigator would.

Conclusion:

Embrace your role as a navigator in the vast ocean of life. By staying true to your values, being adaptable, and seeking guidance, you can chart a course that leads to fulfillment and purpose. Your journey is uniquely yours—navigating it with intention will lead you to the shores of your dreams.

Chapter 14: Embracing Authenticity

Authenticity is a powerful force that allows us to connect with ourselves and others on a deeper level. In a world full of masks and societal expectations, embracing our true selves can be a radical act of courage.

This chapter explores the importance of authenticity in our relationships and personal lives. By being true to ourselves, we create space for genuine connections and foster an environment where others feel safe to do the same.

Authenticity allows us to live in alignment with our values and beliefs. It encourages us to express our thoughts, feelings, and passions without fear of judgment. When we embrace our true selves, we inspire others to do the same, creating a ripple effect of authenticity in our communities.

To cultivate authenticity, we must first engage in self-discovery. This involves exploring our values, passions, and desires, and reflecting on what truly matters to us. By understanding ourselves better, we can confidently express our authentic selves in all aspects of our lives.

Reflection Prompts:

1. What does authenticity mean to you, and how do you express it in your daily life?

2. Are there areas where you feel pressured to conform to societal expectations? How does that affect your sense of self?

3. Can you think of a time when being authentic positively impacted a relationship or situation in your life?

Thought Activity:

Create an "Authenticity Vision Board" where you include images, quotes, and words that represent your true self and aspirations. Use this vision board as a daily reminder to embrace your authenticity.

Conclusion:

Embracing authenticity is a journey of self-discovery and courage. By being true to ourselves and expressing our genuine thoughts and feelings, we can foster deeper connections and inspire those around us. Let your authenticity shine, and encourage others to do the same.

Chapter 15: The Chef

In the grand kitchen of life, we are all chefs, crafting our reality with the ingredients of our words and thoughts. Just as a chef meticulously chooses fresh ingredients, we must select our words with intention, recognizing that each phrase carries energy that influences not only our well-being but also the atmosphere around us.

Imagine standing in front of a stove, the aroma of spices filling the air. Each ingredient you add contributes to the final dish. Similarly, the words we speak create a recipe for our experiences, blending positivity and kindness to nourish our spirits. The act of speaking is not merely a function of communication; it is a powerful act of creation.

Words can enhance or diminish the flavor of our lives. A casual remark, intended as a joke, can unexpectedly sour the mood. It is vital to understand that our speech is not just a sequence of sounds but a powerful force that shapes our world. By infusing our conversations with positivity, we can create a feast of uplifting energy that resonates with ourselves and others.

We often underestimate the significance of our speech and the energy it carries. Every time we speak, we project energy into the world. Why not ensure that this energy is positive? Words possess dynamic power; we are all powerful universal forces capable of creating our realities. Therefore, refrain from speaking negativity into existence. Positive people naturally articulate positive thoughts.

As we engage in dialogue, let us pause and reflect on the impact of our words. Visualize the outcome of our speech as if it were a dish being served. If we accidentally sprinkle negativity into our conversations, we can always adjust the recipe with kindness and understanding. We hold the responsibility to cultivate a loving environment through our words, becoming the chefs of our emotional kitchen.

Reflection Prompts:

1. What words do you often use that may carry negative energy? Consider the phrases you use in casual conversation or self-talk.

2. How does your mood shift after speaking positively versus negatively? Reflect on instances where your words have either uplifted or diminished your spirit and that of others.

3. Can you recall a moment when your words had a profound effect on someone else? Think about the power of encouragement or criticism in your interactions.

Thought Activity:

Create a "Word Journal" to track your speech throughout the week. Document instances of positive and negative language, and reflect on the energy behind your words and their impact on both yourself and those around you. Consider how you can enrich your vocabulary to foster positivity.

Conclusion:

Embrace the power within your words. As you cultivate awareness of the energy you project, strive to foster positivity in your communication. Your words can create ripples, influencing not only your life but also the lives of others. By becoming more mindful of your language, you can transform your internal and external world.

Chapter 16: The Ballerina

In the world of dance, the ballerina exemplifies grace, discipline, and the power of practice. Life, like a ballet, requires us to master our movements, both physically and mentally. Each pirouette and plié is a reminder that our thoughts and words are integral to our performance on the grand stage of existence.

The discipline of a ballerina is not merely about perfecting technique; it is about cultivating a mindset of resilience and self-belief. As we navigate our daily routines, let us embody the grace of a ballerina by refining our self-talk. Each time we engage in positive visualization, we prepare ourselves to tackle life's challenges with elegance and confidence.

When we visualize our goals, we create a mental blueprint that guides our actions. Just as a ballerina imagines her performance before stepping onto the stage, we can picture ourselves succeeding in our endeavors. This mental rehearsal enhances our performance and builds the confidence needed to take the stage of life.

Embracing the discipline of a ballerina teaches us resilience. When faced with setbacks, we can choose to rise gracefully, learning from each stumble. The journey of improvement is not linear; it is filled with ups and downs. Just as a ballerina falls only to get up again, we must cultivate the courage to persist, knowing that our efforts will lead to mastery over time.

Moreover, the practice of mindfulness in our movements—both physical and verbal—encourages us to remain present in each moment. By being aware of the words we choose and the thoughts we entertain, we can foster a supportive inner dialogue that propels us forward.

Reflection Prompts:

1. How do you practice self-talk in your daily life? Consider the language you use when addressing yourself in challenging situations.

2. Can you recall a time when visualization helped you achieve a goal? Reflect on how this technique empowered you to overcome obstacles.

3. What steps can you take to build resilience in the face of adversity? Identify strategies that can help you bounce back from setbacks.

Thought Activity:

Spend ten minutes each day visualizing yourself successfully completing a challenging task. Write a reflection on how this practice impacts your confidence and performance in real-life situations. Consider how this visualization can become a part of your routine.

Conclusion:

Embrace the grace of a ballerina in your life. Through practice and positive self-talk, you can navigate challenges with poise and confidence, transforming your journey into an artful performance. Remember that every step, every word, and every thought contributes to the beautiful dance of your life.

Chapter 17: Reversing Self-Talk

Negative self-talk can infiltrate our minds like an unwanted guest, sowing seeds of doubt and fear. Recognizing and reversing this detrimental dialogue is crucial in reclaiming our inner strength. Our thoughts are powerful energies that shape our beliefs and behaviors; therefore, we must cultivate a mindset that empowers rather than diminishes.

Consider the nature of a thought; it is energy created by our brains, which can be positive, negative, or neutral. This energy flows through us, shaping our beliefs and actions. The more positive energy we foster, the more positivity surrounds us, leading to beneficial interactions and connections. Conversely, negative thoughts can multiply, infiltrating our consciousness and influencing our actions.

When we become aware of negative thoughts, it is essential to challenge them immediately. By transforming these thoughts into positive affirmations, we reclaim our narrative. For instance, instead of saying, "I can't do this," we reframe it to, "I am capable and resilient." Each positive affirmation acts as a shield, protecting us from the corrosive effects of negativity.

Just as we wouldn't allow a persistent weed to take root in our garden, we must not let negative thoughts flourish in our minds. Treat these thoughts as unwelcome intruders and actively replace them with positivity. By doing so, we create a fertile environment for self-love and growth.

Moreover, it's beneficial to create a toolkit of strategies for combating negative self-talk. Techniques such as gratitude journaling, mindfulness meditation, and engaging in positive self-affirmations can fortify our mental defenses. Each day presents an opportunity to reinforce the positive beliefs that nourish our growth.

Reflection Prompts:

1. What recurring negative thoughts do you experience? Identify specific phrases or beliefs that frequently arise in your mind.

2. How do these thoughts influence your daily life and relationships? Reflect on the consequences of negative self-talk on your emotional state and interactions.

3. Can you identify patterns in your negative self-talk? Consider times of stress or change when these thoughts may become more pronounced.

Thought Activity:

Keep a daily journal for a week, documenting instances of negative self-talk. For each entry, write a corresponding positive affirmation to counter the negativity. Use this journal as a tool for self-awareness and growth.

Conclusion:

Recognize the power of your inner dialogue. By actively challenging negative thoughts and nurturing positivity, you can transform your mental landscape and create a healthier mindset. Remember, you hold the pen to your story; write it with kindness and empowerment.

Chapter 18: Finishing Tasks

The act of completing tasks is a testament to our capabilities and a source of empowerment. Each finished task, no matter how small, reinforces our belief in our abilities and propels us toward greater achievements. In this chapter, we explore the significance of follow-through and the joy that completion brings.

Consider the satisfaction that arises when a project reaches its conclusion. This sense of accomplishment can serve as a powerful motivator, encouraging us to pursue further goals. When we finish what we start, we cultivate a sense of accomplishment that fuels further motivation. It is essential to recognize that our efforts, even if they seem minor, contribute to the larger tapestry of our lives.

Embracing the satisfaction of finishing tasks can transform our daily routines. When we approach our responsibilities with intention and commitment, we create a positive feedback loop that encourages us to tackle even greater challenges. Each completed task is a stitch that strengthens our fabric of resilience and self-worth.

Moreover, recognizing the barriers that impede our progress is equally important. Identifying procrastination triggers or distractions allows us to develop strategies that support our journey toward completion. By cultivating a proactive mindset, we can overcome obstacles and find joy in the act of finishing.

Additionally, it can be helpful to practice the art of prioritization. By identifying which tasks are most important, we can focus our energy on what truly matters. Creating a to-do list or breaking tasks into smaller, manageable steps can help streamline our efforts and enhance our sense of achievement.

Reflection Prompts:

1. What tasks have you recently completed that brought you joy? Reflect on the emotions associated with these accomplishments.

2. How does finishing a task impact your motivation for future endeavors? Consider how completion fuels your desire to take on new challenges.

3. Can you identify any barriers that prevent you from completing tasks? Recognize patterns and distractions that may hinder your progress.

Thought Activity:

Choose a task you've been postponing and set aside 30 minutes to focus solely on it. Afterward, reflect on how completing this task affects your mood and motivation moving forward. Pay attention to the satisfaction that comes from follow-through.

Conclusion:

Celebrate the power of completion in your life. Recognize that every task you finish contributes to your growth and self-empowerment. Embrace the satisfaction of follow-through and let it inspire you to pursue even greater challenges.

Chapter 19: Making Small Goals

In the pursuit of our dreams, the significance of setting small, achievable goals cannot be overstated. Just like planting seeds in a garden, small goals yield growth over time, leading us toward larger aspirations. This chapter emphasizes the importance of incremental progress and the joy of celebrating small victories.

Setting small goals allows us to break down our dreams into manageable steps, making them less daunting. Each small achievement serves as a building block, reinforcing our confidence and motivation. By recognizing and celebrating these milestones, we cultivate a sense of accomplishment that propels us forward.

Moreover, making small goals encourages consistency and discipline. By committing to daily actions that align with our aspirations, we create a rhythm of progress that ultimately leads to significant transformation. The journey of personal growth is not always linear, but each small step contributes to our overarching vision.

As we embark on this goal-setting journey, let us remain flexible and open to adjustments. Life is dynamic, and our goals may evolve as we grow. Embracing adaptability allows us to navigate challenges with grace and determination, ensuring that our aspirations remain aligned with our values and passions.

Additionally, visualizing the end result of our small goals can enhance our motivation. Imagine how achieving each goal will feel; allow that emotion to drive you forward. Celebrate each victory, no matter how small, as it brings you one step closer to your larger dreams.

Reflection Prompts:

1. What small goals do you want to achieve this month? Be specific about what you hope to accomplish.

2. How do you plan to celebrate your progress along the way? Consider rituals or rewards that can enhance your sense of achievement.

3. Can you identify any challenges that may arise in pursuing these goals? Anticipate potential obstacles and develop strategies to overcome them.

Thought Activity:

Create a list of five small goals for the month ahead. For each goal, write a positive affirmation that supports your journey. Track your progress and reflect on the lessons learned along the way. Revisit your goals regularly and adjust them as needed.

Conclusion:

Embrace the power of small goals in your life. Understand that each step you take contributes to your overall journey, and celebrate the progress you make along the way. With patience and commitment, you can cultivate the garden of your dreams.

Chapter 20: The Journey Ahead

As we conclude this segment of our exploration, we reflect on the transformative journey of self-discovery and empowerment through words and thoughts. Each chapter has equipped us with tools to navigate our lives intentionally, fostering a mindset that embraces positivity and resilience.

The journey ahead is filled with potential and opportunity. By applying the principles we've learned, we can continue to cultivate positivity, reverse negative self-talk, finish tasks with purpose, and set meaningful goals. Each day presents a new opportunity to practice the art of mindful communication and intentional living.

As you move forward, remember that you are the author of your story. The words you speak and the thoughts you nurture are the brushstrokes that paint your reality. Approach each day with the mindset of a chef, a ballerina, and a resilient farmer, and watch as your life transforms into a beautiful masterpiece.

In this journey, it is crucial to remain open to growth and embrace the lessons that come from both successes and failures. Every experience, whether joyful or challenging, contributes to your unique narrative. By fostering a sense of gratitude for the journey, you can find beauty even in the struggles.

Reflection Prompts:

1. What key lessons have you learned from the previous chapters? Take time to contemplate the insights that resonate most with you.

2. How will you apply these lessons to your daily life moving forward? Develop actionable steps to integrate these insights into your routine.

3. What aspirations do you have for your journey ahead? Visualize the future you want to create and consider the steps necessary to get there.

Thought Activity:

Write a letter to your future self, outlining your hopes and goals. Include affirmations that will guide you on your journey, reminding yourself of the power you hold within. Revisit this letter periodically to reflect on your growth and aspirations.

Conclusion:

Embrace the journey ahead with an open heart and a positive mindset. As you continue to cultivate the power of your words and thoughts, remember that you have the ability to shape your reality and inspire others along the way. Your journey is a work of art—crafted with intention, love, and resilience.

The Journey Continues..

It's important to remember that our journey is ongoing. Each day presents new opportunities to cultivate positivity, reflect on our experiences, and embrace our authentic selves.

The journey to positivity, self-reflection, and authenticity is a lifelong pursuit. Together, let us commit to fostering love and kindness in our lives and communities, creating a ripple effect that transforms the world.

Encourage others to carry the lessons you learned throughout this book into their daily lives. Remind them that they possess the power to create change—not only within themselves but also in the world around them.

In closing, consider how each chapter has contributed to your understanding of yourself and the world. Reflect on the new tools and insights you have gained and how you can apply them in practical ways.

Reflection Prompts:

1. What is the most impactful lesson you learned from this book?

2. How do you plan to integrate these lessons into your daily life moving forward?

3. What steps will you take to continue your journey of growth, positivity, and authenticity?

Thought Activity:

Write a letter to your future self, outlining your intentions for continuing on this journey. Include specific actions you will take and the mindset you wish to cultivate. Seal it and revisit it in six months to reflect on your growth.

Conclusion:

Your journey does not end here; it is just the beginning. By continuing to nurture positivity, reflect on your experiences, and embrace authenticity, you can create a meaningful and fulfilling life. Remember, you have the power to influence not only your life but also the lives of those around you. Let your journey inspire others to embark on their own paths of growth and transformation.

Special Sneak Peek:

Here is a special sneak peek of my Ebook "You Are Your Actions".

You Are Your Actions
By Emem Ossei

44

Chapter 1: Break Free from the Comfort Zone

We've all heard the phrase, "I am who I am." But is that truly accurate? Consider this: a zebra and a horse may look similar, yet their behaviors are vastly different. What truly defines us isn't our appearance or our beliefs, but our actions.

Imagine a mule adorned with a saddle. Does this transformation turn it into a horse? Of course not. Similarly, simply desiring to be something doesn't make it so. To become a "war horse," as the saying goes, one must embody the actions of a warrior. Leadership isn't about titles or positions; it's about leading by example.

Your comfort zone is a gilded cage. It might feel safe, but it limits your potential. Stepping outside of it is uncomfortable, but it's where true growth occurs. Just as a seed must break through the soil to reach the sunlight, you must break free from your comfort zone to flourish.

Why is it so hard to leave our comfort zone?

* Fear of failure: The unknown can be scary. What if you try something new and fail?

* Fear of rejection: Stepping outside your comfort zone might mean putting yourself out there, which can be vulnerable.

* Low self-esteem: You might believe you're not capable of doing something different.

How to break free:

* Identify your comfort zone: What activities or situations make you feel safe and secure?

* Challenge yourself gradually: Start with small steps outside your comfort zone.

* Embrace failure: Mistakes are opportunities to learn and grow.

* Build self-confidence: Believe in your ability to succeed.

* Surround yourself with supportive people: Having a cheerleading squad can make a big difference.

Remember, breaking free from your comfort zone is a journey, not a destination. Celebrate your small wins along the way.

Reflection Prompt: Identify one comfort zone you'd like to step out of. Write down three specific actions you can take this week to challenge yourself.

Chapter 2: Action Speaks Louder

Dreams are powerful catalysts for change, but they are merely blueprints without action. History is replete with figures like Napoleon and Genghis Khan, individuals whose visions ignited empires. What sets them apart? Their unwavering commitment to action.

To be a force in your world, you must channel your energy into purposeful action. Like a sponge absorbing water, you absorb the energy around you. The question is, what do you do with that energy? Do you let it dissipate, or do you transform it into something tangible?

The Power of Habit:

* Understanding habits: Habits are automatic behaviors, often formed without conscious thought.

* Breaking bad habits: Identify habits that hinder your progress and replace them with positive ones.

* Building good habits: Create small, achievable habits that contribute to your goals.

Overcoming Procrastination:

* Identifying procrastination triggers: Understanding why you procrastinate can help you overcome it.

* Time management techniques: Implement strategies like the Pomodoro Technique or time blocking.

* Setting realistic goals: Break down large goals into smaller, manageable steps.

The Importance of Consistency:

* Small steps, big results: Consistent effort over time leads to significant achievements.

* Building momentum: Success breeds success, so keep moving forward.

* Staying motivated: Find your why and connect with your purpose.

Remember, it's not about the size of your dreams, but the ferocity of your actions. Every step you take, every decision you make, is a building block in the structure of your life.

Reflection Prompt: Choose a goal you've been putting off. Break down this goal into smaller, actionable steps. Begin taking the first step today.

Chapter 3: Learn Without Limits

Every experience is a teacher, offering valuable lessons if we're open to them. Don't confine yourself to seeking a single, definitive answer. Instead, embrace the complexity of life and find meaning in every moment.

Consider an apple falling from a tree. It might seem insignificant, but over time, it nourishes countless creatures. Your actions today, no matter how small, can have a profound impact on the future.

It's easy to dwell on the past, but true growth comes from looking forward. Focus on the path ahead, not the road already traveled. Every challenge, every setback, is an opportunity to learn and grow.

The Power of Curiosity:

* Cultivating curiosity: Ask questions, explore new interests, and challenge assumptions.

* Stepping outside your comfort zone: Learning often happens outside of your comfort zone.

* Embracing failure: Mistakes are valuable learning experiences.

Lifelong Learning:

* The importance of continuous learning: Stay curious and engaged throughout your life.

* Setting learning goals: Define what you want to learn and create a plan.

* Finding your learning style: Discover how you learn best (visual, auditory, kinesthetic).

Seeking Mentors and Teachers:

* Finding mentors: Seek guidance from experienced individuals.

* Building a learning community: Connect with like-minded people.

* Teaching others: Solidify your knowledge by sharing it with others.

Remember, there's no waste in life. Everything serves a purpose. Your job is to discover that purpose.

Reflection Prompt: Reflect on a recent challenge. What did you learn from it? How can you apply this knowledge to future situations?

Chapter 4: Create Your Own Reality

You hold the pen that writes your life story. The past is a chapter already written, but the future is a blank page filled with endless possibilities. Don't let past mistakes or regrets dictate your future. Instead, focus on creating a life that aligns with your dreams and aspirations.

Multiplication, not subtraction, is the path to abundance. Every positive action, no matter how small, has the potential to create a ripple effect of growth and prosperity. Reach out, connect, and collaborate. Remember, you are not alone on this journey.

Question the notion of control. Do you believe external forces dictate your life, or do you believe in your own agency? The truth is, you have more control than you realize. Make conscious choices, set clear intentions, and take decisive action.

The Power of Visualization:

* Creating mental images: Visualize your desired outcomes in detail.

* The law of attraction: Believe in the power of positive thinking.

* Affirmations: Use positive statements to reinforce your goals.

Setting Goals and Creating a Plan:

* SMART goals: Set Specific, Measurable, Achievable, Relevant, and Time-bound goals.

* Breaking down large goals: Divide big goals into smaller, manageable steps.

* Creating a roadmap: Outline the steps you need to take to achieve your goals.

Overcoming Obstacles:

* Developing resilience: Build mental toughness to overcome challenges.

* Learning from failures: View setbacks as opportunities for growth.

* Seeking support: Surround yourself with people who believe in you.

Your life is a masterpiece in progress. Embrace the process, learn from your mistakes, and celebrate your victories. Remember, the most beautiful paintings often begin as chaotic strokes.

Reflection Prompt: Write down three affirmations that align with your desired future. Repeat these affirmations daily to shift your mindset.

Don't miss out!

Visit the website below and you can sign up to receive emails whenever Emem Ossei publishes a new book. There's no charge and no obligation.

https://books2read.com/r/B-A-YTCHC-UTJUE

Connecting independent readers to independent writers.

Did you love *The Power of Words and Thoughts*? Then you should read *You Are Your Actions* by Emem Ossei!

Also by Emem Ossei

The Power of Words and Thoughts
You Are Your Actions

About the Author

About the Author

Emem Ossei is a passionate mental health professional with a diverse background in counseling, education, and advocacy. After earning a Bachelor of Science in Psychology from Angelo State University and a Master of Arts in Clinical Mental Health Counseling from Sam Houston State University, he dedicated his career to helping individuals navigate their mental health journeys. His extensive experience spans various roles, including providing therapeutic services to individuals with mental disabilities, working as a case manager for Adult Protective Services, and counseling at-risk juveniles in a residential program.

In addition to his clinical work, Mr. Ossei has contributed to the academic community as a Graduate Assistant in Career Services, where he provided career counseling and assessment interpretation to university students. His commitment to education extends beyond the classroom, as he volunteered as an English teacher at Angkor Tree School in Siem Reap, Cambodia, where he created lesson plans for students of varying English proficiency.

Fueled by a desire for adventure and personal growth, he embarked on a transformative journey through Southeast Asia, backpacking without money while teaching English. This unique experience shaped his perspective on life and deepened his understanding of diverse cultures, resilience, and the power of human connection. His travels not only enriched his professional practice but also inspired a lifelong commitment to advocating for mental health and supporting individuals in overcoming their challenges.

When not immersed in counseling or exploring new places, Emem enjoys sharing insights on mental health, personal growth, and the transformative power of travel through his writing. He believes that every journey, both external and internal, is an opportunity for learning and connection, and is excited to share his stories and insights through his books.